Joy A.

# Tales fron

# MOS



# GULLY

## & Other Australian Poems

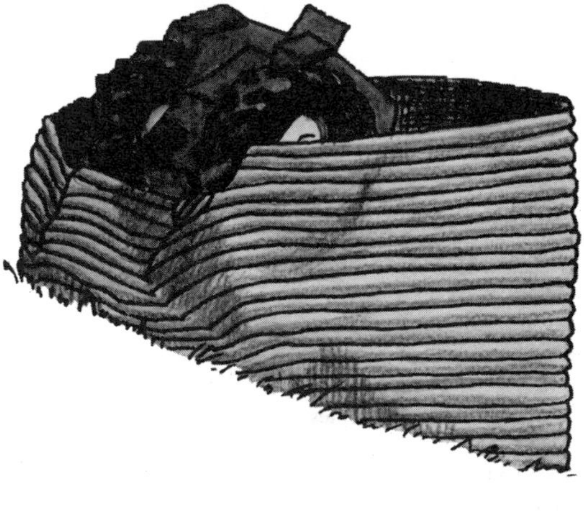

## By the same author

Bess, The Black Orpington Swaggie
Australian Poems That Would Stun A Sheep
More Than Nine Lives
Australian Poems That Would Boggle A Bull

Published by Philip R. Rush
224 Sunny Hills Road
Glen Huon Tasmania 7109



1st Edition March 1998 4000 copies



Printed and bound by The Monotone Art Printers Pty Ltd.
Argyle Street, Hobart Tasmania

ISBN 0 9585443 0 1

*To my wife, Yvonne, for her patience as she listens to all the 'first drafts', and for her constructive criticism.*

*Thanks, also, to Jim McCarter, Ron Woolley, Keith Woodward, Robyn Marmion, Bill Garnham, and others who have been willing to share so many stories with me.*

# CONTENTS

Old Jim's Cows 2
Old Jim's Tractor 5
Old Jim's Football Game 8
Mike's Lagoon 15
Willy-Willies 18
Old Jim's Motor-bike 22
The Bellowing Bull 27
Old Jim's Christmas 31
Shaving 35
She was Fifty, At Least 36
Farmer Jim 37
Bess, The Black Orpington Swaggie 40
Bess, The Black Orpington Swaggie - A Sequel 46
Yes!!! 49
Sunrise 51
A Swarm Of Bees 52
The Party 56
The Slow-combustion Stove 57
Jess - Wounded In Action 58
Disturbed 60
The House of Treloar 61
Atmospherical Problems 66
Blackberries 67
The Rooster 68
The Spirit Of Matilda 70
Hope 71
Possums and Gardening 72

Many Happy Returns ____ 73
The Possum Catcher ____ 74
Home! ____ 79
Dangers ____ 80

Is It True? ____ 82
On Bushwalking In The Western Arthur's, Tasmania ____ 84
Corrugated Iron ____ 88
Pandani ____ 89
The Dunny ____ 90

# INTRODUCTION

Mosquito Gully is a mythical, yet typical, country community in rural Australia. It has a General Store that also doubles as the Post Office, an hotel, local hall, school, church, Fire Brigade shed, and several houses. The local cricket\ football oval is down by the creek, and the surrounding countryside is farmland.

The majority of farms in the area raise sheep or cattle, but there is a sprinkling of wheat farms around, along with some dairy farms on the river flats.

The community has its share of local 'characters', Old Jim being one of the most famous. Most of the farmers are battlers who, like so many farmers throughout Australia, find it a struggle to make a good living from farming, due to the vagaries of the weather, and the fluctuations in commodity prices. However, there is a strong community spirit, and most of the locals have that special sense of humour that is peculiar to Australians, and rural Australians in particular.

Many of the stories related in the following poems are based on real characters, and real incidents, but some have used a little more imagination, and a little less truth than others. For those who have shared some of the stories with me, I thank you; and I trust that all of you will enjoy the poems as much as I have enjoyed writing them.

The majority of these poems have not been published before, but three can be found in two of my other books, "Australian Poems That Would Stun A Sheep", and "Australian Poems That Would Boggle A Bull." This has been done so that the majority of poems on the cassette tape (due for release mid-1998) of "Tales from Mosquito Gully and Other Australian Poems" can be found in this one volume.

# OLD JIM'S COWS

*(This is based on a true, but not unique, story, for the events in this tale have been repeated in many areas throughout our country!*
*The whole community quickly hears of mishaps such as these, for in places like Mosquito Gully, the "Bush Telegraph" is at its most efficient, and very few, if any, incidents are not reported!)*

Driving home from 'who-knows-where' a little while back,
I saw a rather battered cow beside the gravel track:
She looked somewhat the worse for wear, with cuts upon her knees,
As there she stood, a mite bemused, amongst a group of trees.

"You know, I'm sure," I said aloud, "that's Old Jim's Jersey cow;
He keeps a mob in Paddy's place, and she's escaped somehow."
"You'd better go and tell him then," says Yvonne, she's my wife;
"Cattle wandering on the road can cause a bit of strife."

Well, naturally, I agreed with her, and so we motored on.
Jim lived ten mile up the track, just past my brother, Ron.
We hadn't gone a half a mile, when, stone the bloomin' crows!
We found another damaged cow, with blood upon her nose!

She looked a little dazed as well, like she had hit her head;
"Looks like she's got concussion; but that can't be," I said.
"She does look quite bewildered," my anxious wife replied;
"And look, she's got a nasty gash right along her side."

We drove on for a mile or two, and reached McDonald's Hill;
And there we found *another* cow, lying very still
Right across the gravel road - I leant upon the horn,
And, as she slowly looked around, I saw her ear was torn.

"There's something fishy here," I said; and, since I couldn't
pass,
I helped the cow get to her feet, and walked her to the grass
That grew, quite thickly, by the road, then motored on some
more,
And there, a little up the hill, we found cow number four!

She, too, was sagging at the knees, and looking rather crook,
Her eyes were open very wide and had a stary look.
"This poor old thing is seeing stars, and lucky she's alive.
And look! Another stumbling cow; that makes it number five!

We hurried on to tell our friend; and on the way we saw,
Not one or two of Old Jim's cows, but half a dozen more!
A final right-hand turn we made, and reached the old bloke's
gate,
But we could see quite plainly that we'd come a little late!

Old Jim, a glazed look in his eye, was sitting in his truck:
His wife was there beside him; we thought they might be stuck.
But, no! They were not stuck at all - just simply staring back
At a cow that stood beside them on their rather muddy track.

We stopped our car and walked across in time to hear him say,
"Isn't that a cow of ours we loaded up today?"
He gave a start when I replied, "Too right it is, my friend,
You've left a cow along this road on almost every bend!"

"We noticed one along the track with blood upon her face,
Just up from where you keep the cows in Paddy Murphy's
place.
We thought we'd come and tell you, and we've seen a dozen
more -
Next time you load up cattle don't forget to shut the door!

# OLD JIM'S TRACTOR

*(Another true story! It is the "mother" in the poem who told it to me - so how much more authentic can it be?)*

Old Jim had bought a block of land on top of Painter's Hill:
As a spot to fatten cattle this paddock filled the bill.
He put a mob of bullocks there before they went for sale,
And checked them every second day, and thereby hangs a tale.

It didn't happen long ago, 'twas just the other day
That Jim put on his carry-all a biggish bale of hay.
He drove his tractor up the hill to feed his bullock herd,
Where a string of rather strange events unhappily occurred.

As Jim drove past his neighbour's place to turn into his gate,
The bale of hay began to shift, but, jumping off too late,
He didn't have a chance to stop the round and heavy load,
And so he watched the massive bale roll, rumbling, down the
road!

It rolled into his neighbour's yard and crushed the roses there;
It missed the aviary, full of birds, with just an inch to spare!
And, disappearing down the hill, it scattered lambs and sheep,
But worse was yet to follow that would cause Old Jim to weep!

As Old Jim watched the heavy bale careering on its way,
The tractor, too, began to move; and, much to his dismay,
Although he chased as fast he could, the tractor travelled faster,
And through his neighbour's yard it went and headed for
disaster!

Jim watched in anguish as it crashed, and tears came to his
eyes;
He rubbed his hands across his head and looked up to the skies;
But help was not forthcoming: he took a breath or two,
And wandered slowly 'cross the grass, not sure of what to do.

He knocked upon his neighbour's door, but no-one was about;
He took a notebook from his coat, and tore some paper out.
He scratched his head for quite a while, and then he carefully
wrote
A tersely worded, conscience-stricken, most unhappy note.

His neighbour's wife and son came home around a half-past
four,
And straightaway they saw the note that Jim put on the door:
They read it once, they read it twice, and then the mother
spoke,
"I think," she said, "that this must be some silly sort of joke!"

But no! They read the note aloud - "I'm sorry," it began,
"About the tractor in your tank - I'll drop in to explain."
They looked across the yard and saw their battered water tank,
From where the tractor hit the side, continued on, and sank!

"It looks to me," remarked the son, "he's dropped in once
today."
But Jim came round again that night, and said, "Of course, I'll
pay
The cost of a new water tank; I'm sorry for the mess;
But accidents will always be a part of life, I guess!"

The water tank has been replaced, the tractor's good as new;
The garden bed has been restored where once the roses grew.
But gossip travels very fast and, next day, on his gate,
Jim wasn't pleased to find a pair of giant "learner" plates!

# OLD JIM'S FOOTBALL GAME

*(When two rural communities are not far distant from each other, one often finds that competition, especially in the sporting arena, is very fierce. I have played in many games of football where the actual scoring of goals seemed to be secondary to flattening one's opponent!*
*This ferocity, however, does not usually extend beyond the match itself, and the social get-together afterwards makes up for the intense rivalry seen on the field of play.*
*The trophy played for in this game is said to be a boot once belonging to Jack Dyer. Jack was a "no-holds-barred" player of Asutralian Rules football in the Victorian Football League Competition in the nineteen thirties and forties; and few more rugged players ever played the game!*
*This poem has been written to try and portray the strength of feeling that was sometimes engendered between teams. The two communities at war here are Squatter's Ridge and Mosquito Gully, but the same intensity of competition is still seen between many neighbouring townships throughout the land!)*

They're fond of sport at Squatter's Ridge, a settlement outback;
And in Mosquito Gully, too; they'll always have a crack
At any sporting contest that involves some sort of ball:
And, when a challenge they accept, they go in, boots and all!

But any match played nowadays is reckoned rather tame
Compared with what is now recalled as "Old Jim's Football
    Game" -
The annual grudge match held in March before the autumn
    break,
With a perpetual mounted boot and pride of all at stake.

The boot, they say, had once belonged to legendary Jack Dyer,
Who played our National Football Game with courage, strength,
and fire.
The men from Squatter's Ridge had won for six successive
years,
And Jim's Mosquito Gully lads for them held little fear!

But Old Jim's team were sure they'd win, for they'd been
training hard;
A rough and fearsome lot they were, and proudly battle-scarred.
A fitter, tougher mob of blokes not anywhere you'd find,
Although the men from Squatter's Ridge were of a similar kind.

On that last Saturday in March, way back in sixty-five,
I headed off to Squatter's Ridge, a three to four-hour drive.
I had a bit of trouble parking somewhere near the ground,
For folk had come to see this match from fifty miles around!

The paddock where the ground was played was really quite
immense,
Eight to ten chain long and wide, ringed by a barbed-wire
fence.
And, as the crowd increased in size, anticipation grew,
Until the match got underway about a half-past two.

The umpire there was Sandy Jones, but not used much at all,
His only job, it seemed to me, was just to bounce the ball!
And, from the start, this football match was furious and fast,
Whilst in the crowd three fights broke out before two minutes
passed!

Four quarters long the game was set, a half an hour for each,
But two hours solid football was beyond some players reach!
So fifteen men sat on the bench for each opposing side,
And they would all be needed if the start was any guide.

Within the first five minutes not a single score was made,
But three of Squatter's Ridge's blokes were resting in the shade!
Stumpy Smith had smashed his fist when thumping Piggy Rose,
And Woody Best and Doc Mackay each had a broken nose!

Old Jim's team fared somewhat worse, for, still before a score,
Snorter Jack and Buffy Higgs each had a broken jaw!
When Gully's opening goal was kicked by forward Billy Tibbs,
Ridge's full-back flattened him, and fractured several ribs!

At quarter time each team had lost six players from the field,
The score was three goals two a-piece, and each refused to
yield!
After just five minutes break, the umpire's whistle blew,
And soon, both on and off the field, the antagonism grew.

The blood rule wasn't yet in vogue at Squatter's Ridge that day,
And just as well, for had it been, there'd none be left to play!
Every player's uniform was somewhere stained with red,
And even umpire Sandy Jones was cut around the head.

When half-time came, the Squatter's team was just a goal
behind,
Though players fit enough to run were difficult to find!
Yet, after twenty minutes break, some strength returned again,
But still each team took to the field with only thirteen men.

It wasn't long before the pace had faded to a jog,
And so the match reverted to a bruising, painful slog!
When, towards the quarter's end, Shanks Tyson did his knee,
Mosquito Gully's football team had been reduced to three!

Squatter's Ridge were better off, not three they had, but six;
And, with this great advantage, scored three goals through the
sticks!
But Jim was far from finished, and, with his strength immense,
Slammed two of Squatter's Ridge's team, quite fairly, through
the fence!

So, when the quarter ended, the Gully was behind,
And Old Jim knew that further goals would sure be hard to
find.
Ten points down the Gully was, that meant two goals to win;
And Old Jim sighed, and waited for the quarter to begin.

Sandy Jones held up the ball, for this, the final session;
The three Mosquito Gully boys were first to gain possession.
They drove the ball towards their goal, and somehow made a
score,
And Squatter's Ridge's ten-point lead had been reduced to four.

As the ball was relayed to the centre of the ground,
The shouts and yells from all the crowd was heard for miles
around!
But, no matter how they cheered, the score remained the same,
Until the final minute of this famous football game.

The teams were down to two a-piece, and Old Jim had the ball,
The pace had slowed, by all four men, to just above a crawl.
Jim staggered towards Mosquito's goal, the crowd were all
    engrossed,
When Ridge's Nobby Peters thumped him hard into the post.

Nobby grabbed the bouncing ball as Jim was laid out cold,
And kicked it high the other way towards the Ridge's goal:
But Gully's last remaining man was there to intervene,
A strong, but very weary lad, by name of Tim McLean.

The two remaining Squatter's men approached from either side,
And sandwiched him between them both as he kicked high and
    wide;
But, as young Tim dropped senseless down, one Ridge's player
    fell,
And cracked his head on Nobby's skull, as far as we could tell.

And so, with only seconds left, and no-one left to play,
The ball, last kicked by Tim McLean, continued on its way:
It looked like it would miss the goal and finish out of bounds,
But first it had to pass Old Jim, unconscious on the ground.

A sudden hush came o'er the crowd, the silence was complete,
And, as everybody watched, the ball hit Jimmy's feet;
It took a sharp, right-angled turn, and, as the whistle blew,
It bounced between the towering goals, and slowly trickled
    through!

A roar erupted from the crowd, and went on unabated!
The Gully team had triumphed! Their supporters were elated!
Old Jim and youngster, Tim McLean, were cheered by one and
all;
And were the District's toast that night at Gully's Victory Ball.

The local hospital, for weeks, was full of wounded men:
Old Jim, although as tough as boots, he never played again;
For he retired that very night resting in the fame
Of having kicked the winning goal in "Old Jim's Football
Game."

# MIKE'S LAGOON

*(Spooky stories, unsolved mysteries, and reports of unknown creatures are told in many pubs throughout our land. Many are supposed to be based on fact, but are often highly embellished. The ones told in Clancy's Pub at Mosquito Gully are no exception; and long and varied are the wonderful sagas told there, especially after a few drinks on a Friday night!*
*Lagoons, creeks, and waterholes are often the focus of such wonderful tales, and this one is no exception.*
*I will let you judge as to the veracity, or otherwise, of this tale.)*

He was young and from the city, and, perhaps, a little rash,
His attitude, when talking, was confident and brash.
He held no truck with legends, of narguns and the like;
He was our latest schoolie, and he said his name was Mike.

On Friday nights he'd join us for drinks in Clancy's Pub,
And he'd listen to the stories of the blokes out in the scrub:
'Twas many wondrous sagas and myst'ries that they told,
But Michael's verbal rubbishings were something to behold!

No matter what the story, he'd say it wasn't true;
Of even Father Patrick's yarns he was suspicious, too!
But his tongue was at its sharpest and vitriolic worst
Whenever Jim insisted that our lagoon was cursed!

We all knew of the story - how swaggie, Jackie Boon,
Had disappeared, when camping, beside our own lagoon.
And other stories, too, were told, of eerie sounds and light
That people passing our lagoon had heard and seen at night.

It's quite a pretty picnic spot that we frequent by day,
But all, including Mad Dog Max, at night keep right away.
But Mike, he wouldn't have it, would not believe a word
Of stories of the Black Lagoon, what folk had seen and heard.

"Don't talk to me of bunyips, your heads have all gone soft:
It's all imagination, you're irrational," he scoffed.
"I'll camp down there at your lagoon, and take some kids along:
On our return next morning you'll see you all were wrong!"

We tried our best to stop him, but all to no avail:
"Someone has to show you the lies in all your tales!"
So Mike went off undaunted, completely unafraid,
And said he'd show us cowards the stuff of which he's made!

He didn't find it easy persuading kids to go
To camp with him at our lagoon, for most of them said, "No!
You wouldn't catch us there for quids once darkness has
arrived;
Old Jackie Boon the swaggie stayed, and he, poor fella, died!"

"Don't talk such rot!" growled angry Mike. "There's some must
come with me!"
But, from the children at the school, he only mustered three
To go one Friday afternoon and camp at our lagoon.
Mike chose a Friday that would have a full October moon.

Mike left word that he'd be back by noon the following day;
But midday came, and midday went, and then, to our dismay,
Along the road, three frightened boys, their eyes all open wide,
"Our teacher, Mr. Harrison, has disappeared!" they cried.

We took them into Clancy's place, and, when they settled down,
They told us why the three of them had run, non-stop, to town.
"Our teacher, he was telling us that bunyips don't exist;
And, when he talked, the dark lagoon was covered with a
mist!"

"The moon was high, and from the mist we saw this thing
arise:
A monstrous, evil shape it was, and, right before our eyes,
It took our teacher, chair and all, then slowly slipped away;
We're never going there again, not even in the day!"

We searched, of course, for many days, right from that
afternoon;
But not a sign of Mike we found - we named it 'Mike's
Lagoon'.
So all of you good people who come from near and far,
I warn you to believe *each* tale that's told in Clancy's Bar!

# WILLY-WILLIES

*(Old Jim, like so many farmers, finds it hard to keep up with every job that needs doing around the farm. So it often happens, as in this story below, that repairs are carried out to sheds, fences and the like only when time permits, or, as in this case, when one is actually confronted by the task.*
*Willy-willies, or 'dust devils' as they are often called, are regular features of the Australian outback landscape, especially in summer. Usually of small dimensions, these whirlwinds can be quite large and dangerous - as can be seen in the following poem!)*

There's whirlwinds in the Middle East, and twisters in the
States,
But we have willy-willies here, as this sad tale relates:
It must have been December on a fiercesome summer's day -
Old Jim and son were working in his paddock carting hay.

They were carting to the hay-shed that was up beside the gate,
Which was, like many hay-sheds, in dilapidated state.
The wooden posts were rotting and the iron roof was brown,
And many of the iron sheets were in need of nailing down.

Jim saw the sheets and went to get a hammer and some nails,
And left his son to struggle with the few remaining bales.
On his return he told his son to go and shift the cows,
"While I," he said, "will fix the roof on this old shed of ours."

"It's pretty hot," his son remarked, "And you've been carting
hay."
"But there's no wind," Old Jim replied, "to worry me today."
So Jack went off to move the stock while Jim repaired the
shed,
With thoughts of any problems never entering his head.

As he removed a sheet of iron he heard a roaring sound,
And, thinking there was someone there, he slowly turned
around.
It took a moment, maybe two, for him to realise
That a willy-willy was coming straight towards him up the rise.

He had no time clamber down before the wind arrived
And ripped away the sheet of iron, but, somehow, Jim
contrived
To stay secure by wrapping both his arms around a beam,
As, all about, the storm kept up its strange, unearthly scream.

The son looked up from where he was and watched, with great
despair,
The roof, complete with poles attached, rise slowly in the air.
It disappeared behind the hill with Jim still holding on;
His son, of course, raced up the slope to see where Dad had
gone!

When, all red and out of breath, he reached the top at last,
The danger from the willy-willy had well and truly passed!
And, scanning the horizon and fearing for the worst,
He saw a sight that made him laugh as though his lungs would
burst!

Below him, with astonished looks, a flock of ewes and lambs
Were staring, with bewildered eyes, at one enormous dam
Which now contained a hay-shed, like some gigantic boat,
With Jim on top, and, thankfully, the roof remained afloat.

Now I forgot to mention that our hero, Farmer Jim,
For all his fifty-seven years had never learnt to swim.
So here he was, and somewhat bruised, but suffering little harm,
Marooned upon an island roof on this, his outback farm!

Well Jack, his son, kept laughing till he could laugh no more;
He threw a rope to Father, and dragged him safe ashore.
But, next week in his letter-box, with humour raw and dark,
Jim found a wooden farmer on a model Noah's Ark!

# OLD JIM'S MOTOR-BIKE

*(Like many of us, Old Jim is not one to take kindly to change. But every now and again something happens that encourages us to look for a modern alternative to our old ways - as Jim does in this poem).*

On a farm away out yonder,
Where few folk ever wander,
Old Jim had lived for fifty years or more.
He was lean, and tough, and wiry,
And was obstinate and fiery,
But a dinkum Aussie battler to the core!

He had beef and sheep a-plenty,
And his son, a lad of twenty,
Said, "A motor-bike would help us with our stock."
"No, son, you can't beat horses
On hills or watercourses,
Where there's precious little else but sand and rock."

But, in the weeks that followed,
Old Jim's opinion mellowed,
And, maybe, that was due to more than fate.
For his horse, one morning, propping,
Found Jim no way of  stopping,
And he landed on the barbed wire paddock gate.

On being so upended,
Jim's body slowly mended,
But, still angry with the horse that threw him down,
He took his car and trailer,
From the outback of Australia,
And drove for several hours to reach the town.

The bike that took his liking,
To say the least, was striking!
A monster of a bike with lots of chrome.
And so Old Jim acquired
The bike he most admired,
And got into his car and headed home.

And, when at home arriving,
Despite his hours of driving,
He sat upon the bike and switched it on.
His son, who stood beside it,
Said, "Father, can you ride it?"
But, before he got an answer, Jim was gone!

With a roar that split the silence,
The bike, with sudden violence,
Careered across the yard and through the gate.
As it raced towards the mulga,
Old Jim, with language vulgar,
Clung grimly as he waited for his fate.

His son, though none too clever,
Did decide, however,
That, maybe, something really should be done.
He drove the car and chased him,
But the motor-bike outpaced him,
As it headed west towards the setting sun.

Through the mulga branches whipping,
Jim's skin and clothes were ripping
As he struggled to remain upon the seat.
With blood he was bespattered,
And a mob of roos he scattered
From where they rested in the evening heat.

Jim struggled with the steering
As he wildly went careering
Across river-bed, and salt-pan and ravine.
Emus jostled one another
As they hastily sort cover
From Jim upon his murderous machine.

Every bump and corrugation
Caused further aggravation
To the bruised and bloodied body on the seat.
As sense and hope were going,
Jim felt the engine slowing,
Then it stopped - and his journey was complete.

Jim's immediate survival
Depended on his son's arrival,
Who was still negotiating sand, and scrub, and roots.
When he came, a little later,
He was stunned to find his pater
Bruised and battered and unclothed, except for boots.

Still seated, stiff and gory,
On the bike in all its glory,
Jim was senseless, and his son thought he was dead.
But, on listening intently,
He heard father moaning gently,
So he took him home and put him straight to bed.

Jim stayed in that condition
Of the seated, stiff position
For a week upon the bed where he was laid.
And recovery extended
For months before he mended
From that fiercesome motor-cycle escapade.

And no more is there debating
When stock need relocating
As to whether horse or motor-bike is best.
Jim continues using horses
Through the scrub and watercourses,
And the motor-bike has long been laid to rest!

# THE BELLOWING BULL

*(Another true tale, told to me by one of Old Jim's neighbours. If it wasn't so funny it could have been serious!!)*

One cold July evening, Old Jim and his wife
Were watching the programme called, "This is Your Life."
But, since they were weary, there eyes gently closed,
And, there in the lounge room, the two of them dozed.

Soon Jim was asleep and he started to snore,
But his sleep was disturbed by a knock on the door.
When he opened the door the verandah light showed
A couple of blokes who lived just up the road.

"We're on our way back from a party in town,
We saw from the road that your gate's broken down,
And most of your cattle have let themselves out;
We thought you should know that they're roaming about."

"I'm going to bed," said his wife to Old Jim.
"You three are enough to get the cows in."
She went to bed, and the three men together
Went out in the winter's most miserable weather.

With two blokes to help him, it wasn't that hard
To lock all the beasts in the old cattle yard.
Old Jim thanked his mates, and refused a lift back,
"It's only a couple of shakes up the track."

He thought to himself, as they drove down the hill,
"If I go through the paddock, I'll be quicker still."
So he turned himself round to climb over the fence,
But fell from the top with a terrible wrench.

He strained his left ankle, his back, and his knee,
And, as well, lost his torch, and he now couldn't see;
So, wet through and freezing, he started to crawl,
There was no other way that he'd get home at all!

When his wife woke up later, Jim wasn't in bed;
She thought for a moment, then to herself said,
"I bet he's gone off with his mates for the night
To have a few drinks." And she turned off the light.

But she just couldn't sleep; in the paddock nearby
Some animal kept up a piteous cry.
She thought to herself, "Some poor heifer or steer
Is stuck in the mud, and Old Jim isn't here!"

She sought to ignore it, but however she tried,
There was no chance of sleep while the animal cried.
So, being soft-hearted, she gave in at last,
And prepared to go out in the cold winter's blast.

She thought that the roar had a desperate note,
As she put on her gumboots and waterproof coat.
She picked up a torch, and set out in the sleet,
Not finding it easy to stay on her feet!

Gamely she struggled on treacherous ground,
Heading ever towards the unhappy sound
That wailed in the wind, in the sleet and the rain,
A cry of an animal suffering in pain!

At last she could see it, ahead in the light,
And, oh! How surprised she was at the sight!
For there was Old Jim calling out in distress,
And how long he'd been there was anyone's guess!

"I tried to crawl home after having a fall,"
He said to his wife. "Now I can't move at all."
She managed, somehow, to get back to the house
With her wounded and miserable, shivering spouse.

Old Jim has recovered, his back's doing fine,
But there is, unanswered, a question of mine.
If his wife had known that the cry came from him,
Do you think that she still would have rescued Old Jim?

# OLD JIM'S CHRISTMAS

*(There are many hardships to face on an Australian farm, drought, floods, fire, being some of the more obvious ones. Often these hardships are faced alone, at other times they are tackled by the community as a whole.*
*Such threats are even more disturbing when they come at times of the year that are meant to be joyous times, and family times, such as Christmas.*
*This is a story about just such a time.)*

The year had been long, and the year had been dry,
With no decent rain since late in July.
And now, close to Christmas, the harvest was down,
And the grass in the paddocks was withered and brown.
Jim looked at his stock, they weren't sleek any more,
The condition of most a bit forward of store.
Old Jim wiped his brow with the back of his hand,
Then, adjusting his hat, the horizon he scanned.
On the distant blue hills, through the shimmering haze,
Was a large plume of smoke where the bush was ablaze.
"No threat to us here," he muttered aloud,
As he gazed at the faraway, billowing cloud.
"Unless a strong northerly blows up, of course,"
He said as he patted his faithful old horse.
"But then, me old girl, it'd take half a week
To get to our boundary down there by the creek."

He flicked with the reins and returned to the house,
And there he was greeted by Gladys, his spouse:
"Judy and Alan have arrived with the boys;
But the baby's asleep, so don't make any noise.
You promised to get them a tree when they came
To put up at Christmas; I guess one the same
As we've had every year. Can you get me one in?"
"I know what you want," Jim replied with a grin.
"A branch of a cherry, the native one here,
I'll see that you'll have one this arvo', my dear.
But first for some lunch - have something to eat,
And get out, for a while, from this dreadful heat."

It was later that night, and the boys were in bed,
When Alan, Jim's son, to his father said,
"There's a smell of smoke in the air tonight,
And the moon is tinged with a reddish light,
There's fire on the hills that I saw today,
There's every chance of it getting away;
For the wind is up, and it's northerly, too,
Is there anything more I can help you do?"
"No! The trailer's right, and the firebreaks done,
I've completed the fire preparation, son.
I'm feeling weary, I've been busy today;
I think it is time that we all hit the hay."

By the following day Jim was ill at ease,
For the fire had spread on the northerly breeze,
And was racing across the desolate plains,
And never a chance of a sudden rain.
On the day before it was Christmas Eve,
Old Jim and his son decided to leave
And join in the fight to control the blaze
That had burnt, unchecked, for so many days.
As they started the ute and prepared to go,
Old Jim heard the voice of his grandson, Joe,
Who said to his Pa, with a hint of alarm,
"Will the fire keep Santa from reaching the farm?"
"I'll think he'll be here, and he won't forget
There are kids on the farm - he hasn't missed yet!
We hope to be back before Christmas day;
And meanwhile, lad, we can hope and pray
For the wind to change and the rain to fall,
Or it could be a difficult time for all."

Old Jim and his son went away to fight,
And they didn't come home at all that night.
And on Christmas Eve they were still away;
And so, at the end of a worrying day,
Young Joe went inside, and on bended knees,
Prayed for some rain, and a southerly breeze.
But the weatherman gave a prediction bleak,
And, later that night, fire jumped the creek;
And, to Jim's dismay, it went racing again
Through the withered grass on the windswept plain.

Then the captain announced to his weary troop,
"It's back to the house, where we'll all regroup.
It'll give us an hour, or a little more,
Before it approaches the homestead door."

As the men drove back through Old Jim's farm
The northerly died, and an eerie calm
Proclaimed the arrival of a smoke-filled day:
And, to everyone's amazement, the skies were grey!
As the south wind blew, and the raindrops fell,
The exhausted men gave a thankful yell,
And a soot-stained Jim, with his reddened eyes,
Was greeted by the noise of his grandson's cries.
"I prayed for rain, and the south wind, too,
And Santa Claus came, and so did you!"
He leapt in the arms of his Grandpa Jim,
And his Pa shed a tear as he cuddled him.
He turned to the men and his family there,
This weather-beaten bloke with the snowy hair;
"Strange things have happened in my life before,
But nothing like this has surprised me more.
I'm all overcome, don't know what to say,
'Bout the miracle that's happened this Christmas Day.
But I thank you all, and the captain, too,
And the very best of Christmases to each of you!

# SHAVING

*(Old Jim doesn't like change. When he heard that the double-sided razor blades he had used all his adult life were soon to be discontinued, he had to do something about it!)*

Old Jim is pushing sixty, and set in all his ways,
Including, I might tell you, the way he always shaves!
He hates electric shavers - they don't cut fine enough,
And, he likes to mention, his stubble's far too tough!

He's not so ancient-fashioned as to use a cut-throat still,
But the modern, single, narrow blades he reckons are a pill!
"The one I use I've had for years, the best one ever made;
The old-time safety type that needs a double-sided blade!"

Old Jim dropped in the other day; he had some morning tea;
And, as we chatted on and on, Old Jim confides in me;
"Those razor-blades I always use are not made any more,
I looked for them in all the local supermarket stores."

"But that won't stop me using them, I've got a little stack;
Enough for three or four more years, about a dozen packs.
And soon, I'm told, a mate of mine is heading overseas,
And in London you can buy a pack for ten or fifteen p!"

"To save me hunting everywhere, to save a lot of strife,
He can buy me thirty packs - enough for all my life!"
I've heard of forward planning, but this sure takes the biscuit;
And thirty packs through Customs? You think his mate will
risk it?

But enough of idle chatter, and just ‘twixt you and me,
There is something in the future that I’d really like to see.
Once Jim has got his lifetime stock of safety-razor gear,
Is for his wife to sweetly ask Old Jim to grow a beard!

## SHE WAS FIFTY, AT LEAST

*(One way of getting peace and quiet!)*

She was fifty, at least,
Her skin was all creased,
And the wrinkles with dirt were accented.
She lived with her clan,
Fifteen kids and her man,
And their noise all the neighbours resented.

Her sixteenth was due,
And arrived right on cue,
And was duly to mother presented.
Soon after she’d come,
A young, first-time mum,
Asked how chaos at home she prevented.

“With all those young frights
You’d have terrible nights.”
But old mother a cure had invented:
“An aspirin to each,
Off with hearing aid switch,
And I sleep very long and contented!”

# FARMER JIM

*(Old Jim fancies himself as a top sheepdog trainer. I have seen some of his dogs at work, and have to admit that they respond to Jim's whistles and calls to perfection. However, there are things regarding working stock he still has to do himself.)*

Now Jim he was a farmer and a proper one at that,
He wore the proper clothing and a fine Akubra hat.
He was into raising cattle and a thousand head of sheep,
And he lived in Mosquito Gully where the hills are pretty steep.

He was an expert horseman, but his work dogs were his pride,
And rarely was he seen without a canine by his side.
They'd run along beside his horse, or sit up in the ute,
And each was willing, if required, to work the meanest brute.

With "way back" call, or "sit", or "here", each dog would work
with zest;
They'd move the cattle, ewes, or lambs wherever Jim thought
best.
They'd cut a cow out from the herd, or yard some angry steers,
While Jim would watch, with sense of pride, as he had done for
years.

Despite the skill of all his dogs, of Rover, Red, and Blue,
There was a job he'd never trained his working dogs to do.
He'd tried, of course, to no avail - but still believed, some day,
He would have a dog that helped to take this chore away.

Each winter's day, at lambing time, Jim would check the ewes;
Full-woolled they were, and every year he'd quite a number
lose.
Sometimes a sheep, when wool was wet, would finish upside
down,
And there would die, unless Jim came, and turned it right way
round.

This turning sheep annoyed Jim more than almost any task,
With paddocks steep, and driving sleet, and winter's icy blast.
If he could only train a dog the struggling ewes to turn,
He could stay inside the ute and wretched weather spurn!

And then one day Jim called on me with Rover at his heel,
He wanted me to go with him, and said, "It's just unreal;
I've never seen a dog before do what this dog can do;
I've taught him now, at flamin' last, to turn a stranded ewe!"

I asked him how a dog could get a sheep back on its feet.
Jim replied, "Just climb aboard." I sat up in the seat.
He drove me to a paddock where old Rover would perform;
His ageing Queensland Heeler dog, more than a little worn.

I watched Old Rover run to where a ewe lay on its back,
And then I saw what Jim had taught, what startling, little knack
The dog had learnt, as to the sheep it ran and chewed its ear!
The sheep, reacting violently, got to its feet through fear!
.................................................................................................
Old Farmer Jim's still raising sheep, and most successful, too;
But still he has a winter's chore, and one he hates to do:
It's turning full-woolled ewes about, it nearly makes him weep,
For Rover was the only dog that learnt to turn a sheep!

# BESS, THE BLACK ORPINGTON SWAGGIE

*(This poem had its beginnings in a short anecdote I heard on the radio one Sunday morning. It led me to thinking about the idea of chook becoming a swaggie, and taking off for a life "on the track."*

*The concept so appealed to me that I wrote a full-length novel about "Bess, The Black Orpington Swaggie" which the ABC published in 1993.*

*The book itself, although obviously a fantasy to a certain extent, was also semi-historical, for many of the characters Bess met on her journeyings were real people, and the stations that she visited were real stations, most of which are still in operation today.*

*The events she became involved in, such as an outback picnic race meeting at Eromanga, and droving cattle down the Birdsville Track with that Prince of drovers, Bill Guyder, soon after the Second World War, are also based on real events.*

*This poem, however, is somewhat more fanciful, but I daresay the old-timers of Mosquito Gully remember Bess very well indeed!)*

She was raised on a farm in Dimboola, surrounded by Wimmera wheat;
She knew icy frosts in the winter, she suffered the long summer's heat.
A little, black Orpington chicken, she grew to a good-laying hen,
But her thoughts often turned to adventure, away from her wire-netting pen.

Each morning the Farmer's son, Arthur, would let her out into
the yard,
Along with the rest of the layers, (for whom she had little
regard);
For Bess, as this Arthur had named her, was a tough,
independent, young chook,
And she'd spend many hours gazing westward, with a dreamy,
faraway look.

"My future is not as a layer, I'm sure there are more sights to
see
Than I could ever imagine, and the life on the road is for me."
So she gathered a few, basic items, wrapped up in a calico bag;
And tied the bag up in a blanket - a little, black Orpington's
swag.

Thereafter each night she would settle, not in with the rest of
the hens,
But under the cart on the axle, for this was the means to her
ends;
At last came the night she was wanting, the family went out in
the cart;
As she bumped along on the axle, excitement rose high in her
heart.

The family was off to tin-kettle a young couple who'd recently
wed,
And they waited, of course, till they reckoned the couple would
be well in bed:

So off in the darkness they trotted, unaware that Black Bess
underneath,
Was having a ride - had she had them - that would loosen all
of her teeth!

So the couple was duly tin-kettled; then Arthur discovered the
hen -
"Hey! Look!" he exclaimed, most astonished, "Black Bess has
got out of her pen!"
'Twas then that Black Bess nearly panicked, but she kept her
swag hidden from view;
And Arthur said, "Might as well leave her, she looks like she's
stuck on with glue!"

When they'd finished tin-kettling the couple, they all drifted
back to their homes,
The Gardiner's, the Smith's, and the Griffiths'; the Shepherd's,
the Menzies' and Baume's.
But Black Bess never reached the old farmhouse, she jumped
off at the road leading west:
With her swag, with its blanket and billy - she started her
journey with zest.

Through the small hours of morning she plodded, and then, at
the breaking of day,
They saw her nearing Jeparit, two travellers from over Perth
way:
No longer a jaunty, young chicken, her feet were now blistered
and raw;
And she'd wrapped them up in blue denim, to stop them feeling
so sore.

One of the travellers stopped her, and spoke with a voice kind
and true,
"And what are you doing, young chicken? And where are you
travelling to?"
But Bessie could not speak too clearly, and the one word that
she answered back
Was a feebly drawn-out husky "Arthur" as she stumbled along
on the track.

There was drought in the wheat-belt that summer, and meals
were a problem each day,
But she worked her way all round the country, from Quilpie, to
Wentworth and Hay.
She swept up the crutchings in woolsheds, she helped press the
wool into bales,
She even helped out with the muster, way out in west New
South Wales.

She tramped through the year 'forty-seven, the year of the
Mallee mouse plague,
She remembered it all very clearly, though my recollections are
vague.
She ate rabbit stew with the swaggies, and often repaid with an
egg;
For an Orpington proud was young Bessie, she'd vowed she'd
not steal food or beg.

After two or three years in the Outback, she headed for
different terrain;
It was up in the mountains I met her, with the cattle up on the
high plain.

She told me she often missed Arthur, to Dimboola one day
she'd return;
But she still had a sense of adventure, she still had a lot more
to learn.

By now she was really quite famous, Black Bess the Orpington
chook;
And the shearers and drovers all knew her, she was often
employed as their cook.
She learnt to play fiddle and banjo; and many a station outback,
Would ask her to play at their dances each time she blew in
from The Track.

She travelled from Wave Hill to Derby, and then on to
Kimberley Downs.
She travelled all over Australia, keeping out of the really big
towns.
For some years I heard nothing of her; I thought she'd by then
must have died,
But late in the fifties I saw her, there was no mistaking her
stride.

I pulled up beside her and chatted, and, strike me! She knew
me by name,
This now battered, old, greying Bessie, still plucky, courageous
and game.
She still had her bluey and billy, the same that she'd taken that
day
From the kitchen she'd known as a chicken, when she lived
over Dimboola way.

She said, with a voice sounding weary, she'd now had enough
of The Track,
With the flies, and the dust, and the tourists - "too many now
travel outback."
She said that she'd do one more circuit - to say fond goodbyes
to her friends,
Then settle back home in Dimboola, with Arthur and some of
his hens.

And so we are now in the nineties, I've not seen old Bess now
for years,
But sometimes, when oldies are chatting, I a rumour
occasionally hears
About a black Orpington swaggie they'd met somewhere out on
The Track;
But I doubt that I'll e'er again see her, I doubt that she'll ever
come back.

.......................................................................................................

*(When this poem was first broadcast on the radio, the following verse finished the poem).*

So Arthur, I heard of your 'phone call, on "Australia All Over"
you said
That you'd last seen young Bess at a tin-bash; she never
returned to the shed:
But Arthur, I hope you are listening; your Bess was a dinkum
'true-blue',
And intended, when journeys were over, to return to Dimboola
- and you.

# BESS, THE BLACK ORPINGTON SWAGGIE - A SEQUEL

*(Since writing the novel "Bess, The Black Orpington Swaggie", many people have asked me am I going to write more of her adventures. That is undecided, but I did write this poem as a sequel to the one on the previous pages).*

I was making my trip to the saleyards, as I do every fortnight
or so,
When I met an old mate from the mountains, a stockman
retired long ago:
We leant on the sliprail together, and yarned of the old days
again,
When he mentioned to me that he'd seen her; the Swaggie
Black Orpington hen.

"She's living up there in the mountains, with Sally, her grand-
daughter chook;
She'll never go back to Dimboola, she's housebound and looks
pretty crook.
But her memory is sharp as a razor, and she loves having visits
from friends."
He gave me directions to find her, beyond where the Dargo
Road ends.

Last weekend I went up to see her, and my eyes became misty
and blurred
As I gazed at old Bess in her rocker, this old and remarkable
bird:

No more would she carry her bluey, no more would she wander
Outback;
No more would the drovers and stockmen meet Bess, with her
swag, on The Track.

As I thought of her life as a swaggie, my face gained a faraway
look,
But I soon was brought back to the present, by Bess, the
redoubtable chook:
With sparkling, bright eyes she addressed me, and said, in a
voice loud and clear,
"Don't stand there and wallow in pity - just wake up, young
man, and sit here!"

I sat down beside her and chatted, and she told me the rest of
her tale,
How, late in the sixties, she'd struggled, for her legs were
beginning to fail.
How she longed to get back to Dimboola, but her grand-
daughter Sally had said,
"You know how hot summers distress you; why don't you retire
here instead?"

Bess spoke of her first years with Sally, how she yearned to
return to the life
That she'd led for so long with enjoyment, along with some
trouble and strife.
But her restlessness gradually left her, her Wanderlust feelings
have gone;
Though she misses her roving companions, so many who now
have passed on.

And so, as each year quickly passes, her visits from friends have grown less;
So, if you are travelling the mountains, you should try and visit old Bess.
She lives on the High Plains with Sally, with nephews and nieces nearby;
Her house is out on the horizon, just there where the land meets the sky!

# YES!!

*(A little while ago I read an article in the paper about the responses people give to questions on interview shows on television and radio. The writer made the comment that, although the word 'no' is still widely used, the majority of questions answered in the affirmative were rarely answered with just a simple 'yes'.*
*The writer went on to comment that we may lose 'yes' altogether from our language!*
*I thought that I would put this article to the test, so last week I did some interviewing of my own in our local township. This is the result.)*

They say that language changes, and our words they come and go,
Some disappear through lack of use, I guess.
But a word we'll have for ever is the toddler's favourite "No!"
But its opposite's at risk, and that is "Yes!"

I must admit this idle thought had never crossed my mind,
That such a word as 'yes' would fade away;
But a writer in the paper said it's pretty hard to find
A person who will answer 'yes' today.

This statement so intrigued me that I thought it would be fun
To prove this writer's statement incorrect.
So, when I went to town last week, my random trial begun,
But I wasn't really sure what to expect.

I first ran into Johnno, and I said to him, "Gidday,
I hear you lost a cow the other night."
He rubbed his chin, then answered in his usual, wordy way,
"Whoever told you that, me lad, was right!"

He told me all about it, but, at last, I said, "Goodbye."
And continued on my way quite resolutely.
Then, meeting Fred, I asked him, "Is it true you've learnt to fly?"
He said to me, quite proudly, "Absolutely!"

"I've bought a little Victa, come fly with me some time."
But I didn't want to listen any more:
For I'd seen our local sergeant, "There's a lot, I hear, of crime."
And he replied succinctly, "That's for sure."

It was getting close to lunch-time, so I went to buy some food,
"May I have a cup of tea, and pie and sauce?"
And the girl behind the counter, in a manner rough and rude,
Loudly answered, with a sharpish tongue, "Of course!"

Four times I'd asked a question where the answer should be 'yes',
And no one used that word in their reply.
But I wouldn't give up easily, I'm a stubborn bloke, I guess,
So I thought I'd give my test a further try.

Another dozen questions, all I got was "that is true",
Or "I reckon", "So I hear", or "That's a fact";
And at every "non-yes" answer my disappointment grew,
"Yes" seemed to be a word my cobbers lacked.

At last I drove, defeated, to my home out in the scrub,
And met my wife outside the kitchen door.
I said, "What say we have a meal down at the local pub?"
My wondering wife replied, "Whatever for?"

"I've got no hidden reason, just feeling rather down."
My wife replied, "I'd have to go and dress.
But I wouldn't mind to go and eat a meal with you in town;
So if you care to wait the answer's YES!"

I grabbed her and I kissed her, I danced her round the house;
I held her in a long and fond caress:
For, at last, my search was over, thanks to my darling spouse,
When she answered with a sweet and gentle 'yes!'

## SUNRISE

*(We are fortunate to live where we can watch the sun rise over the eastern mountains. Every morning seems to bring a different kaleidoscope of colour as the sun reappears to bring in a new day!)*

The blackness softens into grey upon the eastern sky,
And heralds to the wakening world that dawn herself is nigh.
Soon grey is tinged with hints of pink, diffused with golden
thread;
And, as I watch, the sky erupts in clouds of fiery red.
While heavens ever brighten with extravagant display,
The sun majestically appears to welcome in the day.

# A SWARM OF BEES

*(This poem was first published in "Australian Poems That Would Boggle a Bull." It is repeated here because it should also be on the spoken cassette which is to be released mid-1998.*
*'Jack', the hero of this tale, is a 'gunna', "I'm gunna do this, I'm gunna do that", but that was often as far as it went, and the jobs were left undone. Jack preferred to spend a lot of his spare time in his large shed. In his shed was a pit, the type you can drive your car or truck over so it can be serviced underneath. Unbeknown to Sue, Jack's wife, Jack had a little hollowed out recess at the bottom of this pit, and there he kept a good supply of cans and stubbies for himself and his mates.*
*This poem could also be called "The Dangers of Drink", an obvious title, you will agree, on reading the poem.*
*The story was told to me by a South Australian, who vouches for its veracity. I'll leave it up to you to decide on its truth, or otherwise!)*

Jack was always going to do the jobs around the house
That were requested regularly by Sue, his patient spouse;
But, somehow, things were rarely done, for Jack preferred
        instead
To ask a mate or two to share some drinks down in his shed.

As Sue was working in the house one fine November day,
A largish swarm of bees arrived, and seemed content to stay
Within the wall that stood between the kitchen and verandah:
Since Jack was slow in tackling them, it raised his spouse's
        dander!

For several weeks the bees remained, and really were a pest,
But long-wed Jack was expert at ignoring Sue's requests.
At last, exasperated, Sue gave Jack an ultimatum,
"It's either me or bees that go - I tell you, Jack, I hate 'em!"

"They've followed me about the house, they've fallen in the stew;
They've interrupted all this week the things I've gone to do.
I won't be home till evening, Jack; I'm off to town today,
If there are bees when I get back, I'll leave you straight away!"

These words he heard caused Jack to shake, he knew his wife was serious,
For this was no benign request, but a command imperious!
Not wishing for his wife to leave, he answered Susan's warning,
"I'll see the wretched swarm of bees is all removed this morning!"

When Susan left, Jack called his mate, "I've got a job to do;
And I'm not sure I'll get it done without some help from you."
Steve came around to help his friend, but first they had a drink,
And then he said, "It's easiest to smoke them out, I think."

They lit some old and oily rags and put them in the vent.
The acrid smoke stirred up the bees, but few, if any, went!
So Jack and Steve went to the shed to have a further think,
And, since the day was pretty warm, they had another drink!

It took a drink, or maybe three, before ideas struck.
"I know," said Steve. "We'll use the hose, they'll drown with
any luck."
But all they did was flood the floor, and stain the kitchen wall;
They didn't drown a single bee, not a single bee at all.

Back to the shed and a drink again; then other schemes they
tried:
But the bees stayed put within the walls, and not one insect
died.
At last Jack thought of a clever plan, to remove the window
frame,
And vacuum up the swarm of bees before his Susan came!

Late in the afternoon it was when the window frame came out;
And Steve and Jack, their hopes up high, gave an early victory
shout!
"This plan of ours can't fail," said Steve, "These bees are soon
to die."
"No doubt about it," Jack replied. "We're brilliant, you and I!"

The drinks were beginning to take effect, and both were three
parts gone
When they stuck the pipe in the swarm of bees and switched
the vacuum on!
Then it was only a matter of time, and the bees were in the
bag;
Their ploy, it seemed, had done the job far better than smoky
rags!

But, though they were caught, the bees weren't dead, and the
vacuum fiercely roared,
As the angry bees kept up their din - they couldn't be ignored!
So Steve came up with the bright idea to try and gas the lot,
And down on the floor beside the stove they found the
connecting spot.

Lying flat on the floor they pushed the hose of the vacuum on
the pipe
That brought the gas to the stove inside, and then the time was
ripe
To turn the gas and the vacuum on, and this they did with glee;
And a loud explosion rent the air, and the room was filled with
bees!

Five minutes it was, at the very least, before the men came to
And surveyed the sad and sorry scene, and their consternation
grew,
For the door was split, and the vacuum gone; but what was
worst of all,
Dead bees were plastered inches thick on ceiling, cupboards
and wall!

It was then that Susan came home from town, and their knees
began to knock,
But Sue, surveying the dismal scene, recovered from the shock
And laughed and laughed both loud and long at Steve, and her
husband, Jack;
With hair all singed, and their beards, too, and shirts blown off
their backs!

Jack painted the walls, and the ceiling, too, and mended the kitchen door;
And the jobs to be done around the house aren't put off any more.
But, down at the pub, both he and Steve are very much ill at ease,
For someone always asks them both how to shift a swarm of bees!

## THE PARTY

*(A feast I threw for a few friends of mine!))*

I found an old log by the side of the track
That I thought I could cut to add to the stack.
I cut it in lengths with my trusty old saw,
But found, to my chagrin, a termited core.

This eaten-out centre I threw to one side;
The now homeless termites had nowhere to hide.
I sat on a stump just yards from the mess:
A thrush soon appeared in his sombre, grey dress.

This feast soon attracted a family of wrens,
And a Thornbill arrived with a half-dozen friends.
A Flame Robin, too, with his fiery red breast
Flew down from the tree that sheltered his nest.

Ignored by the throng, I sat for an hour
Watching the birds the termites devour:
No longer annoyed that the log had proved rotten,
My woodcutting job I'd all but forgotten!

# THE SLOW-COMBUSTION STOVE

*(Cheap to run, cosy, nostalgic; the slow-combustion stove, still much used in rural areas, does have a certain charm. Nonetheless, it can be a little temperamental, as this poem shows.)*

We've got a slow-combustion stove that serves us well enough,
But sometimes, when it's in the mood, it makes things pretty
tough:
Oh! mostly it decides to work the way we want it to,
When heating up the water or a saucepan full of stew.

But, when we're in a hurry, the stove plays little tricks,
The fire, instead of flaring, smoulders on the driest sticks!
And if we want to cook a roast when visitors arrive,
It often doesn't start to heat till sometime after five!

It causes some frustration to the lady of the house,
And a smidgeon of concern to her devoted spouse.
And when a tribe of daughters come for an extended stay,
The water, heated by the stove, is lukewarm every day!

Although we clean it regularly, it sometimes likes to smoke,
And triggers off the fire alarm - just for a nasty joke!
Yet other days it's perfect, both clean and fiercely hot,
And that's the time it isn't needed by us all, as like as not!

We like our old combustion stove, for all its funny ways;
It keeps us warm and cosy on the coldest winter days.
And, when it causes trouble or refuses to behave,
We've always got the frypan and our little microwave!

# JESS - WOUNDED IN ACTION

*(A good, working farm dog is a valuable asset to a farmer, and often a 'good mate' as well. It pays the farmer to look after his dogs, and many hate to see them hurt.*
*Jess, a black-and-white kelpie cross, is one such dog. The yards she was working in at the time of this story have gates that are closed with hooks and chain, each hook like the sharp end of a butcher's hook.*
*I was working in the yards this day, and hence the poem!)*

We were drenching some sheep in the yards by the shed and
the dogs were helping us out.
I was using the gun in the race when my mate called for help
with an ear-splitting shout;
"Your dog has got caught in the hook of the gate, it's made a
great hole in her side."
I put down the gun and jumped over the fence, and hoped that
my dog hadn't died.

Jess was alive, as alive as could be, but the hook had her
screaming in pain:
My mate had tried hard to take out the hook but Jess kept on
biting again.
I grabbed my best dog by the scruff of her neck and lifted her
up for a look,
This loosened the chain, and I carefully pulled, and extracted
the damaging hook.

She'd a hole in her thigh underneath her back leg, and the
wound looked angry and raw;
How deep was the hole we couldn't quite tell, but Jess wasn't
well, that's for sure.
She staggered away with a limp and a moan and sat in the
shade of a tree;
I went to her there and I patted her head, and she looked very
sadly at me.

I left her and hoped she'd recover all right, but I wasn't too
hopeful, I guess;
And, as drenching continued, I didn't say much - I kept
worrying over my Jess.
By the time we had finished she'd got on her feet and was
gingerly walking about,
And, ten minutes later, attempted to run, for the sheep were all
coming out.

She couldn't resist the chance to work sheep, and she helped
move them back down the road;
Although she was keen, she wasn't herself - the effect of her
wound really showed.
She went for a swim in the dam on the way, but we soon knew
that something was wrong;
It must have been water had stung on her wound for she didn't
stay in very long.

She came out with a whimper and looked most perplexed, but
soon started running around:
She followed the sheep for most of the time, but she kept her
sore leg off the ground.
And then, as she tired, we lifted her up and let her ride home
on the tray,
She didn't object, although when she's fit, she likes to keep
running all day.

I thought that I'd have to take Jess to the vet, but she's looking
much better this morn;
Although she can't jump as she usually does, I guess it's still
sore where she's torn.
But one thing I'll say, it's amazing to see how quickly my dog
has come good;
But I noticed this morning she kept well away from the hook
just as much as she could!

## DISTURBED

*(Another short poem that reflects another event that often occurs as I am gathering firewood!)*

I split the log and there he lay,
Stunned by shock and light of day;
A frightened lizard, fat and grey.
I watched, entranced, and hoped he'd stay,
But, when I moved, he sped away.

# THE HOUSE OF TRELOAR

*(It was in the early nineteen-sixties, and I had been appointed to a one-teacher school in the country. My first board was good, but, when the family went on holidays, I was assigned different board, and the farmhouse I lived in for a week was less than satisfactory, as this sad tale relates.*
*This poem was first published in "Australian Poems That Would Stun A Sheep", but is also included here, for it is also most likely to be on the cassette of "Tales from Mosquito Gully.." which is due for release in mid-1998.)*

At their farm I arrived
About quarter past five,
And that's when I first had misgivings.
I'd been offered some board,
And the rent could afford,
So accepted their bed with thanksgiving.

I'd not been there before,
And gasped as I saw
The filthiest yard I'd seen ever.
Mud, compost, manure,
Plus junk, made a sewer
Look like a fresh mountain river.

Through this unwholesome sludge
The farm animals trudged,
And the children played happily in it.
And there, at the door,
Stood the wife, Pat Treloar,
Calling out that she'd just be a minute.

She pulled on some boots,
Gave some guffawing hoots,
And tramped over, still roaring with laughter.
"Come in, luv!" she bawled,
So meekly I crawled
From my car, and stepped gingerly after.

When I ventured inside,
I very near died,
The smell in the house was appalling.
And the yard seemed to creep
Through the back door, and seep
Into each crack and chink in the flooring.

"Would you like cup o'tea?"
Pat bellowed at me,
And no reason I found for refusing.
From the teapot she drew
A foul-smelling brew,
That was not to my taste or my choosing.

As I sat with my drink,
Pat stood at the sink;
She prepared all the food as I eyed her.
All the peelings and skins,
All the bottles and tins,
She tossed through the window beside her.

Soon after being fed
I went off to bed,
Away from the rubbish disgusting.
’Twas an old wooden bunk;
And the room, full of junk,
Could have done with a clean and a dusting.

But the air was less rank,
And, though it smelt dank,
The room was both peaceful and quiet.
And the bed, although old,
Proved to keep out the cold,
Once I pulled back the covers to try it.

Not feeling to bright,
I switched off the light,
And tried to forget what I’d eaten.
For our dinner had been
A stew, most obscene;
My stomach, though tough, was near beaten.

I was hoping to sleep,
Have a rest, long and deep,
But this was a hope soon exploded.
Once the room became black,
There emerged from a crack
Some beasts, and my peace was eroded.

As they scurried nearby,
I decided to lie
In the dark, and try to ignore them.
But of this was no chance,
For they made an advance
On the bed-posts, and started to gnaw them.

The noise was so great
I became most irate,
And I turned on the light to deter them.
But they steadily sat,
Those abominable rats;
I was greatly repulsed by these vermin.

I ran quickly outside,
For some fresh air I cried;
But, alas, the air was polluted.
What with pig sties nearby,
Rotting cabbage piled high,
My stomach felt most convoluted.

My distress was intense
As I leaned on the fence,
And my stomach gave in altogether.
But, at last, I returned
To the bedroom, and yearned
To be gone from this farmhouse for ever.

I survived there a week,
But my future looked bleak,
Had I stayed at that house any longer.
I'd enough of the rats,
And the squalling of brats,
And the smell which grew steadily stronger.

So I made some excuse
To this family obtuse,
And drove to my home in the city.
I soaked in the bath
For an hour and a half,
To get rid of the stench and self-pity!

I was able to find
Board of different kind,
And very happy I was, to be sure.
And I now seldom speak
Of that horrible week
I endured in the house of Treloar.

# ATMOSPHERICAL PROBLEMS

*(We regularly hear or read about the hole in the ozone layer, and how it can damage us by allowing more ultra-violet rays through the atmosphere.*
*We are also told that this 'hole' has been largely caused by mankind releasing too much of certain chemicals into the air. Things such as these are not always easy to understand - as this poem suggests!)*

They told me that over our part of the world there's a massive
great hole in the sky,
But, when I looked up, I saw unbroken blue, not even a crack
could I spy.
So I went off to visit this scientist bloke, who tried very hard
to explain
How this hole in the sky isn't quite what it seems, then he had
to explain it again.

"You're sayin'," says I, with a quizzical look, "that this hole in
the sky isn't real.
It's a thinnin' of some sort of ozone-y bit, that'll take us a
century to heal?"
"That's it," said the boffin, and then he went on to tell me how
crook it can be
If we let out from our 'fridge or other machines some stuff that
he called CFC.

"Yer know," he then says, "them things on yer face, them spots
and the dark, little mole;
They'll only get worse, and not just for you, if we can't get rid
of that hole.
The thinner it is, the more burns we get from some ultra-violin
sort of rays;
Not only when there's a clear sky overhead, but even on
overcast days."

Well, this fair shook me up, but then he goes on and talks
about greenhouse and stuff.
I tell yer, by now, me brain was clogged up, I really had
listened enough.
I can't see no greenhouse up there in the sky, or holes for the
rays to leak through;
And I'll bet you a dollar, or Perth to a brick, that neither can
any of you!

## BLACKBERRIES

*(I always carry a notebook and pencil, and I try to write something every day. This was written as I was down by our creek, wondering what I was going to do about the blackberries!)*

Succulent blackberries, juicy and sweet;
And blackberry jam for me is a treat.
Blackberry pie is equally grand -
But why must blackberries grow on our land?

# THE ROOSTER

*(People are always telling me stories. Stories that have been bandied around the bush for years, stories that would make your heart ache, stories that are poking fun at someone or other, and stories such as this one, guaranteed to be true.*
*I have found that many of these 'true' stories are to be found throughout the bush, and are more like 'urban myths', except, in these instances 'rural myths'.*
*This one may be true, and maybe not, but it makes a good yarn, anyway.)*

I hear a lot of stories about happenings on the farm;
Some are rather lurid, and some have special charm.
But I heard this story lately, and hesitate to say
That it's entirely truthful, but I'll tell it anyway!

It happened that a couple thought they'd like to raise some
chooks:
They consulted all their neighbours, and they read the proper
books.
They built a lovely chookhouse, and a wire-netting run;
For that is how the job of raising chickens is begun.

They bought a handsome rooster, and a dozen hens as well;
And things were doing nicely, as far as they could tell.
They soon had eggs a-plenty, and a broody chook or two,
So it wasn't very long before the flock of chickens grew.

A month or three along the track they thought they'd like to try
Some freshly-grown chicken-meat; the one they chose to die
Was a tender little rooster, but, not sure of what to do,
Husband wrung the rooster's neck, and pretty gently, too!

The fowl collapsed, and hung its head, and seemed devoid of
life,
So husband took the corpse inside and gave it to his wife.
She, gallant soul, then plucked the bird, and put it in the 'fridge,
And then what followed next, they say, is true, it's 'ridgy-didge'.

'Twas later, when the time had come their dinner to prepare,
The wife, on opening up the 'fridge, could only stop and stare!
For there the rooster, which she thought was well and truly
dead,
Was not a corpse upon a plate, but standing up instead!

She didn't shut the 'fridge again but called her husband in,
And, when he saw the bright-eyed bird, he gave a sheepish
grin!
"The neighbour said to use the axe, then let the body drain;
But I'm not sure that I could kill this rooster once again!"

His wife agreed, and said to him, "The bird is naked now;
It's sure to die unless we keep the poor thing warm somehow."
And so for weeks around their yard, for want of something
better,
The resurrected rooster wore a knitted woollen sweater!

# THE SPIRIT OF MATILDA

*("Waltzing Matilda" has a special meaning to many of us. We like to think we have a close connection to our outback history, our pioneering past. Even those born and bred in the depths of the great Australian cities often feel a deep affinity to the rugged, dry interior of our land.*
*This poem extends these thoughts just a little further.)*

He may have been a vagabond, a rogue, or petty thief,
And might have worked occasionally by way of light relief:
But Banjo's famous swaggie is an Aussie figure grand,
The quintessential battler of our great and wondrous land.

A man content with life he was; of independent bent,
Who managed peacefully, alone, no matter where he went.
He cooked and ate a simple fare, he drank his billy's brew;
And, if a jumbuck chanced along, he'd have a bit of stew.

He dressed for comfort, more or less, he was no stylish fop,
He had no permanent address, at night he'd simply stop
Beside a creek or billabong, his swag beneath his head,
Or, during rain and thunderstorms, he'd camp inside a shed.

He kept his distance from the law, he wanted no dispute,
And rarely acted in a way that might bring ill-repute.
He'd known the ups and downs of life, and never took a poke
At other chaps' misfortunes - he was a gentle bloke.

When trouble did confront him, at peace beneath a tree,
He felt condemned unfairly by each of troopers three.
He sprang into the water - in moments he was gone,
But the Spirit of Matilda eternally lives on.

The ghost of Banjo's swaggie has called from down the years,
Awakening the spirit that was in our pioneers.
Although we're mostly city-bred, we're Aussies through and
through,
And like to think that we, ourselves, are independent, too.

We dream of days departed, of life upon The Track,
And yearn for simple solitude somewhere away out back.
We hear from distant memories the Bush's haunting call;
For the Spirit of Matilda is deep within us all.

## HOPE

Our water-tanks are nearly dry,
When struck they all sound hollow.
High overhead the cloudy sky
Gives hope that rain might follow.

The weather-man predicted showers,
Although they would be scattered.
I watch in vain through morning hours,
My hope is all but shattered.

The afternoon brings darker skies,
And hope has life injected.
A heavy shower justifies
My hope being resurrected.

# POSSUMS AND GARDENING

*(When we shifted from the mainland to Tasmania, we looked forward to establishing a lovely cottage garden. Our dreams, however, have been put on hold by the delightful, yet destructive, possum population around our house.)*

We started growing roses, angel white and blushing red,
But the possums came and ate them - we grew geraniums
instead!

The geraniums were hardy, and it took till early May
For the possums to attack them, much to our dismay!

No geraniums or roses, so pansies were the go,
For someone said the possums would let the pansies grow.

But no-one told *our* possums; the pansies soon were gone.
But, in spite of all these setbacks, the garden struggled on.

Then we heard that fuchsias were possum-proof and tough;
But the possums loved the fuchsias, and they couldn't get
enough!

And yet, by trial and error, we found what possums hate;
Lavenders and daisies were flowers they never ate.

I know it looks peculiar, but the only plants we grow,
Are every sort of lavender, and daisies by the row!

# MANY HAPPY RETURNS

*(This is a true story about a gardener who trapped the possums that were attacking his fruit trees, and took them far away!)*

My mate, he's got a garden, and a lovely one at that,
A place where one can sit and think, or stop and have a chat.
There are many sorts of flowering plants, and fruit trees in, as well,
But who benefits the most from these is difficult to tell!

You see, he's got a problem, for possums live nearby,
And they like to come and visit, and give his fruit a try.
So he's got a trap and sets it in the garden every night,
Then goes outside and checks it in the early morning light.

He's caught a dozen possums that have feasted on his fruit,
And he takes them to the forest in his rather battered ute:
Some miles he drives away from home before he sets them free,
And they usually scramble quickly up the nearest sturdy tree.

But, just a little while ago, although he wasn't sure,
He thought the possum that he'd trapped had visited before.
So he put a spot of paint upon the possum's coat of brown
Before he put it in the ute and headed out of town.

It took a week, I think he said, before the brute returned,
And managed to get caught again, you think it might have learned
To keep away from possum trap; but how far up the track
Do you have to take a possum before it won't come back?

# THE POSSUM CATCHER

*(Another possum story, and a true one, at that! I know it's true, for, although I am somewhat embarrassed to admit it, I am the teacher in the story.*
*This poem was first published in "Australian Poems That Would Stun A Sheep", but is included in here because it is most likely to be on the cassette tape "Tales from Mosquito Gully..." that is to be released in mid-1998.)*

He had finished Teachers' College,
And his head was full of knowledge,
But it wasn't quite sufficient for what now had come about.
All his higher education
Did not help the situation,
He'd a possum in the chimney and he couldn't get it out.

For the bulk of his existence
He'd been very little distance
From the borders of the city and the comforts that it brought.
Now he ws a country teacher,
And could hear the wretched creature
Scrabbling in the bricked up chimney where 'twas obviously
caught.

No Psychology or History
Was a help. It was a mystery
How a possum could be rescued from behind a bricked-up
hearth.
Late at night, and early morning,
Both his wife and he woke, yawning,
As the possum, scratching loudly, sought to find an exit path.

"I'm sure the possum's weaker."
'Twas his wife who was the speaker;
To her husband she was talking as he came home late from
school.
Well, the thought of possum lying
In the chimney, then expiring,
Was too much for both these people, it seemed pitiful and
cruel.

"We must save him, that is certain,
Ere he rings the final curtain."
But 'twas not for noble reasons that the rescue would be made.
For the thought of odours rotten
Coming from the chimney bottom,
Was enough to see that rescue plans would not be long delayed.

So the problem that existed
Had no answer that was listed
In a College course, or covered by a Bachelor's Degree.
So with all his mental vigour,
The schoolteacher tried to figure
How to move the curs-ed possum from the chimney to a tree.

But no answer was forthcoming,
And it sounded like the drumming
Of the possum in the chimney was much weaker to the ear.
"I'll just have to up and feed him,
For we cannot really leave him;
And I'll ask the local farmers how to get him out of here."

Now it happened that a neighbour,
Looking upward from his labour,
Saw the teacher silhouetted on the schoolhouse roof next door.
He was hanging, rather grimly,
By his right hand, to the chimney;
The astonished neighbour waited just to see what was in store.

So the neighbour watched intently,
As the teacher, very gently,
Began dropping bits of bread and fruit straight down the
chimney black.
Then he carefully descended
From the roof-top, and intended
To go inside the schoolhouse, but the neighbour called him
back.

So the poor, embarrassed teacher
Told the story of the creature
Trapped in the bricked-up fireplace behind their bedroom wall.
The neighbour said, with eyes a-twinkle,
"You need a fishing-line to winkle
Out that possum from the chimney if it's had a nasty fall."

Not approving this suggestion,
The schoolteacher went to question
All the farmers in the district how to set the possum free.
"Fill the chimney up with water,
Shouldn't hurt the bricks and mortar,
Then the possum, floating upwards, can be put into a tree."

"Drop a rope so he can grab it."
"Set a trap like for a rabbit,
Tie it on a piece of string and catch him in its iron teeth."
"Get a piece of fencing wire,
(Number eight, but nothing higher),
Long enough to reach the possum in the chimney underneath."

"Spin it round and round quite quickly,
Since the possum's feeling sickly,
It won't move, and you will catch it when the wire sticks in its
fur."
"Take a ferret, and attach it
To a string, and he will catch it."
"Knock the bricks out and extract him, then replace them as
they were."

Now the teacher, with his problem,
Had the mickey taken from him,
And he knew it, but the possum was still trapped behind the
bricks.
When he reached home, night was falling,
And he heard his partner calling,
"The possum's on the roof-top and he's heading for the sticks!"

Now the teacher, disbelieving
That the possum now was leaving,
Climbed up onto the housetop just as fast as he could race.
But the possum was much quicker,
He could almost hear it snicker
As it, diving down the chimney, grinned back up at teacher's
face.

It could scamper up the chimney
Very easily, very nimbly;
And the teacher, red-faced, panting, tried to grab it by the tail.
But the possum kept retreating,
And the teacher's loud entreating
Could not entice the possum from inside its so-called gaol.

It was getting close to midnight
When the teacher, in the moonlight,
Climbed up on to the roof again armed with a concrete block.
On the chimney he then set it,
And the possum, when he met it,
Knew the chimney now was sealed with a very heavy lock.

But this saga had not finished,
For the interest, undiminished,
In the story by the locals went for ever on and on.
And for many months thereafter,
With their faces creased with laughter,
They would ask the blushing teacher had his possum problem
gone!

# HOME

*(A common sentiment, and one I wrote after being away from home for only four weeks!*
*And, yes, I think I can truthfully say I have done, or encountered, all things mentioned in the poem below!)*

I've camped on the Murray, and up on the Range;
I've camped up in Queensland and down at the Grange.
I've hiked in the Flinders, sat by the Barcoo,
I've cooked, in camp ovens, some fine Irish Stew.
I've swum in the Snowy, I've been out to sea,
I've drunk many gallons of strong billy tea!
I've weathered a cyclone, I've seen a few floods,
I've travelled some trails that were three feet of mud!
I've walked on a hundred of bush-walking tracks,
And stood on my share of three-cornered jacks!
I've fished the odd river, I've climbed a few peaks,
Been away for a night, or a couple of weeks!
I've coped with the dust-storms, the wind, and the heat,
And walked many miles with blistered, sore feet.
I've wandered the desert, I've hiked through the snow,
There's not many places that I wouldn't go!
But, no matter whenever, or where I may roam,
I'm always, yes, always, so glad to be home!

# DANGERS

*(I was brought up in the city, but my heart was, and still is, in the bush. I live above the beautiful Huon Valley in Tasmania, surrounded by magnificent views. Our property is covered with natural bush, and the wild-life abounds.*
*Some of our visitors are not too keen on some of our smaller 'creepy-crawlies', but I would prefer them to living in the city any day!*
*Hence this poem.)*

I live in the bush and enjoy it no end,
And many a morning and evening I spend
Walking up tracks and scrambling up rocks
That traverse and lie in the bush on my block.
Visitors, too, sometimes happen along,
And hear, with delight, the various songs
Of fantail and robin, of whistler and wren,
And even a firetail is heard now and then.

But some of our guests are not at all keen
To venture too close to this idyllic scene.
"There's hundreds," they say, of unpleasant creatures,
Like spiders and scorpions, bullants and leeches;
Jackjumpers, snakes, mosquitoes and ticks.
Some of these bites can make people sick!
I'll stay where it's safe in my city or town
Where few of these creatures are running around!"

Oh! I've had the odd bite from a bullant or two,
And a tick on my body I find's nothing new.
One snakebite I've had, and a bee sting or three;
I've lost count of the leeches I've taken off me!
But the city, I reckon's a riskier place;
There's a myriad of dangers that one has to face!
At street intersections, in subway and mall,
There's perils I don't like confronting at all!

I don't wish to be caught in the stainless steel jaws
Of the city's self-opening and self-closing doors!
Or stuck between floors in a broken-down lift
That, though you press buttons, refuses to shift.
And pedestrian crossings! They're largely ignored
By the cars and the trucks as they bellow and roar,
All anxious to be at where-ever on time -
You'd think that to step on a crossing's a crime!

There's the press of the people that jostle and rush -
They don't care at all if you're caught in the crush!
And when evening approaches, and light starts to fade,
Shifty-eyed characters stand in the shade!
It's not safe, I'm told, in the city at night,
Especially on streets with inadequate light.
No! Give me the bush where an odd bite or two
Is better than what all you townies go through!

# IS IT TRUE?

*(The weather has always been a fascination to all sorts of people, and predicting the weather had become an art form well before Weather Bureaus came into existence.*
*Everyone, it seems, has their own way of predicting the weather, both for short-term and long-term forecasts. Aching limbs, the behaviour of various creatures, the look of the moon, in fact, almost anything that changes shape, behaviour, position, or whereabouts is used in the 'freelance' science of weather-forecasting.*
*When, on a recent radio broadcast, I asked listeners to send in their own way of predicting the weather, the range of methods was astonishing!*
*I have listed a few of the methods that I have known about for many years, you are at liberty to add a list of your own on the small, blank space at the end of this poem - or send them to me - my address is in the beginning of this book!!)*

I've heard it said that if you see a ring around the moon,
The chances are that it will rain, and, maybe, very soon.
And if the moon's a crescent, and it lies a certain way,
Im told that rain will bucket down, and probably next day!
And if you see black cockatoos, or hear their mournful call,
Then everyone can rest assured that rain is sure to fall!
The only question I would ask to each and all of you,
On each of these predictions is simply, "Is it true?"

When currawongs leave mountains high and head towards the
plain,
I'm told it means that autumn's gone, and winter's here again.
And if the summer's long and hot, and very dry as well,
The winter will be very tough, or so some people tell.
And I've been told by certain folk, with accents long and grave,
That they can say when floods will come by how some ants
behave!
And other persons say that ducks predict a deluge, too,
But I would simply say to each this question, "Is it true?"

They tell me if a possum has a coat both rich and black,
We're sure the winter will be cold a little down the track.
When morning skies are brilliant red we'll have a rugged day;
And when the kookaburras laugh then rain's not far away.
Red skies at night assures us all tomorrow will be warm,
But if the swifts are on the wing there'll be a thunderstorm.
Now I'll admit that what I've said is really nothing new;
But of each one, however old, I'd still ask, "Is it true?"

........................................................................................

*HERE'S THE SPACE FOR YOU TO WRITE YOUR OWN FAVOURITE METHODS OF PREDICTING THE WEATHER!*

# ON BUSHWALKING IN THE WESTERN ARTHUR'S, TASMANIA

*(I do enjoy bushwalking! I have been bushwalking for years, and have hiked across many places, both in Tasmania and on the mainland.*
*However, as the years have passed, packs have become a good deal heavier, and mountains much steeper, not to mention that I have become somewhat older, yet, in some ways, no less foolish! Take, for example, this bushwalk that my mate, Ron Woolley, and I did just recently. We climbed the Western Arthur Range in Southwest Tasmania, a walk rated 'hard', but should have been rated 'x'!*
*I actually began writing this poem as I struggled up the steepest section of our climb. I wrote it in the notebook I always carry with me, but, on this occasion, I'm not sure its extra weight was worth it!!)*

My socks are soaked, my trousers, too,
My singlet's damp, my shirt wet through;
My hips are sore, my back is gone,
But, doggedly, I soldier on.
My shoulders ache, my knee's in pain,
To climb up mountains is insane!

The bitter wind is icy cold,
And pierces bones now worn and old.
My mate ahead calls, "Not far now!"
Not that I trust him anyhow.
We climb through hail, and sleet, and rain,
And then the snow sets in again!

We struggle up the mountain track;
I hear, nearby, a nasty crack.
I stop and check my spine to see
If what had cracked had not been me!
I'm still intact, though very sore,
I'm not sure I can walk much more!

We stop and rest our bones a while,
My mate can even raise a smile!
"You know," he says, "Next Thursday, Phil,
On our return it's all downhill!"
I don't tell him I couldn't care,
I just reply a simple, "Yeah!"

We start again our wretched climb;
My stomach says it's eating time.
But, "No," says Ron. "We'll reach the top
Before we have our dinner stop."
My hunger pangs will have to stay
Till some time later on today!

My neck is strained, my calves are tight,
And Ron turns round, "Are you all right?"
"I'm fine," says I. "And how are you?"
"A little sore, but I'll get through."
"We're mad," I say: and Ron agrees,
And pushes past some stunted trees.

The both of us need several rests
To calm our over-heaving chests.
We puff and pant, then on we go;
I'll never reach the top, I know!
But then, at last, we're at the peak!
But I've no breath to even speak!

We sit and eat a welcome lunch.
And then Ron says, "I've got a hunch
It's only just an hour or so
To where the camp-site is, you know!"
But Ron has made a small mistake -
It takes three hours to reach the lake!

We set up camp, and then collapse,
And Ron brings out some folded maps.
"Tomorrow, if the weather's good,
There's two more mountains that we should
Climb up and see the splendid views."
My body shudders at the news!

Next day it rains, we stay inside,
And everything that should have dried,
That we'd left hanging on a tree,
Is still as wet as wet can be.
So we play cards for half the day,
And hope the rain will go away.

Next morn the weather's not too bad;
A little better than we've had.
We walk up here, we walk up there,
And spend some time to stop and stare
At all the marvellous views around
That in the Arthur Range abound!

At last we struggle home again,
Repeating all the aches and pain
That comes from carting massive packs
Upon Tasmania's mountain tracks.
But I forget the tortuous path
When soaking in a welcome bath!

And so, when later in the year,
My mate, with grin from ear to ear,
Says, "Want to come and walk next week
To such-and-such a mountain peak?"
"Of course!" I say. "We're pretty fit;
A walk like that won't hurt a bit!"

# CORRUGATED IRON

*(The ubiquitous corrugated iron! Invented by some bloke in England back in the 1850's, this item has become one of the great symbols of rural life in Australia. Its versatility is legend, and its lifespan remarkably long.*
*Everyone in the country seems to know of some unusual use of corrugated iron, and this poem lists but a few.)*

Corrugated iron! What a marvellous invention!
Although I doubt it ever was the purpose or intention
Of the bloke who first invented it in eighteen-fifty-three,
(Or somewhere back about that time, the date's eluded me),
That corrugated iron should be used so many ways!
I reckon that he thought, maybe, back in those early days,
That the iron would be used for rooves, and take the place of
thatch,
Although it's far more likely to produce a nasty scratch!

But nowadays how versatile this iron has come to be!
Just take a look around the place and you will surely see
A range of modern structures such as water-tanks and sheds,
Chicken coops and aviaries, and even simple beds!
And corrugated iron has been used for country halls,
And often used for stables with innumerable stalls!
And pig-sties, too, and garages; a rusty-looking fence -
The variety of uses is really quite immense!

You'd find the outdoor dunny could be corrugated, too;
And once I saw a corrugated, rickety canoe!
Kennels, chimneys, flues, and yards, a rather rustic gate;
And corrugated pizza ovens I've even seen of late!
People wait in corrugated shelters for the bus;
And these can be erected with a minimum of fuss.
Now you might think I've written a most impressive list,
But I can tell you surely there are many things I've missed!

# PANDANI

*(The Pandani, or Giant Grass Tree* {Richea pandanifolia} *is endemic to Tasmania. It is a striking plant, found in the wet forests of mountains and south-west Tasmania.)*

Under sun and under star,
Silent sentinels bizarre,
Watchmen of the bush they are,
Pandani.

Dressed in modest skirt of brown,
Single-legged, with emerald crown,
Never smile and never frown,
Pandani.

High up on the alpine plain,
Through winter snow and driving rain,
You'll never hear these plants complain;
Pandani.

# THE DUNNY

*(Some memories for those who had an outdoor dunny!)*

We had an outdoor dunny,
And it wasn't very funny
To go out the back to use it on a freezing winter's night.
Through the rain we'd go a-dashing,
And through puddles we'd be splashing
With our gumboots and our coats on, and a rather feeble light.

When we reached our destination
We had no inclination
To stay in the little building any longer than required.
There were things that made you wary
Such as spiders, fat and hairy,
And other horrid creatures one's inventiveness inspired.

The situation worsened
For a child, or timid person,
If the torch or flickering firelight of the hurricane lamp expired.
We'd end up feeling wretched,
And utterly dejected,
And we wished we'd not been drinking just before we had
retired.

They tell me time is healing,
But I reply, with feeling,
That this rather cliche-d statement is not altogether true.
For not for love or money
Would I want an outdoor dunny
In the place of what we now have; an indoor, flushing loo!